D1209239

DOLLAR BILL ORIGAMI

Jane Yates

WINDMILL BOOKS

Published in 2017 by Windmill Books, an Imprint of Rosen Publishing
29 East 21st Street, New York, NY 10010

Developed and produced for Rosen by BlueApple*Works* Inc.
Creative Director: Melissa McClellan
Managing Editor for BlueApple*Works*: Melissa McClellan
Designer: T.J. Choleva
Photo Research: Jane Reid
Editor: Kelly Spence
Craft Artisans: Eva Challen (p. 8, 10, 12, 14, 16); Jane Yates (p. 18, 20, 22, 24, 26,28,30)

Photo Credits front cover left Valentina Razumova/Shutterstock; front cover right Samuel Borges Photography/Shutterstock;
Title page background Attitude/Shutterstock; TOC, back cover ronstik/Shutterstock; title page, p. 4, 6 – 31 Austen Photography;
page tops Svetlana Lukienko/Shutterstock; p. 4 top mama_mia/Shutterstock; p. 4 bottom Africa Studio/Shutterstock; p. 5 middle
Satanevich/Shutterstock; p. 5 bottom Atlaspix/Shutterstock

Cataloging-in-Publication Data

Names: Yates, Jane.
Title: Dollar bill origami / Jane Yates.
Description: New York : Windmill Books, 2017. | Series: Cool crafts for kids | Includes index.
Identifiers: ISBN 9781499482263 (pbk.) | ISBN 9781499482270 (library bound) | ISBN 9781508192794 (6 pack)
Subjects: LCSH: Origami--Juvenile literature. | Dollar, American--Juvenile literature.
Classification: LCC TT872.5 Y38 2017 | DDC 736'.982--dc23

Manufactured in the United States of America
CPSIA Compliance Information: Batch #BW17PK: For Further Information contact Rosen Publishing, New York, New York at 1-800-237-9932

CONTENTS

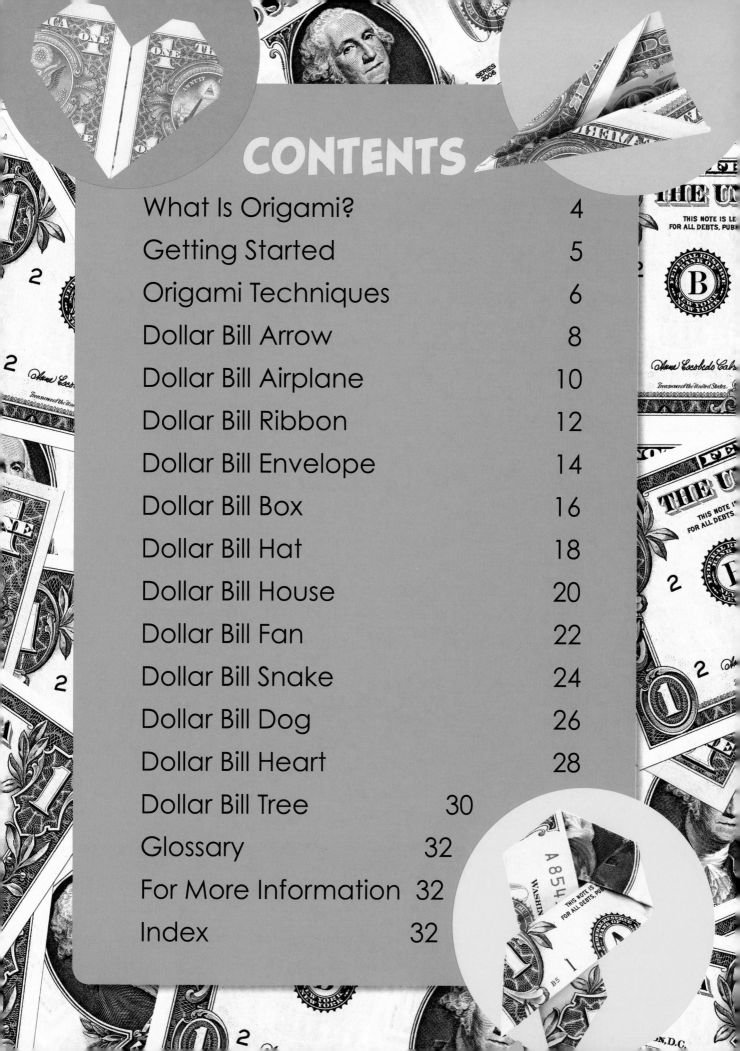

WHAT IS ORIGAMI?

Origami is the art of folding paper into different shapes. Through folds, a flat, **two-dimensional** paper can be transformed into a **three-dimensional** work of art. The art of origami is believed to have started hundreds of years ago in Japan. In Japanese, ori means "to fold" and kami means "paper." A person who practices origami is called a folder. Some origami projects involve just a few simple folds. More **elaborate** designs can take much more time and skill to complete.

DOLLAR BILL ORIGAMI

Origami is a popular art form around the world. Using dollar bills to fold origami is especially popular in the United States. Think of creative ways you can show off your origami skills. For example, at a restaurant, you can ask your parents to leave a server's tip folded into a simple origami shape.

Did You Know?

Paper was invented in ancient China. The Chinese used **pulp** made from bark and a plant called hemp to create sheets of paper. Over time, people began to fold paper, including paper bills, to create different shapes. Today origami is a popular craft for people of all ages and skill levels.

GETTING STARTED

The only material you need to create dollar bill origami is paper money! You can use real dollar bills or play money. It is best if the paper bills are new, but you can work with old bills, too. A coin is a handy tool to crease your folds. When you work with real money, try not to tear the bills. Wash you hands well after folding money. Dollar bills that have been used have been touched by many people.

DOLLAR BILL

QUARTER COIN

PLAY MONEY DOLLAR BILL

A Note About Measurements

Measurements are given in US format with metric in parentheses. The metric conversion is rounded to make it easier to measure.

Tip

It is best to work with new, crisp dollar bills!

ORIGAMI TECHNIQUES

Origami is made using different kinds of folds. Valley folds, mountain folds, outside reverse folds, and pleat folds are all needed for the projects in this book. Follow the following steps to create each kind of fold. You can practice making the folds with scrap paper before making dollar bill origami.
Ask an adult if you need help.

VALLEY FOLD

A valley fold creates a bend in the middle of the paper. It makes a V-shape.

1. To make a valley fold, lay the paper on a flat surface.
2. Bend the bottom of the sheet upward to meet the top edge.
3. Line up the edges. Make sure the corners are lined up, too.
4. Hold the edges together with one hand.
5. With the other hand, pinch a sharp crease.

Valley fold

MOUNTAIN FOLD

A mountain fold is made in the opposite direction of a valley fold. It looks like a pointed tent. Instead of folding the bottom of the paper up, fold the top down. Then follow the same steps used to make a valley fold.

Mountain fold

Spread out pleat fold

OUTSIDE REVERSE FOLD

This fold allows the paper to change directions. It is often used to make the head of a bird or the feet of animals. The outside reverse fold wraps over the rest of origami project in the direction of your choice.

PLEAT FOLD

A pleat fold it made up of several valley folds and mountain folds. It looks like an accordion or a staircase. Make a valley fold followed by a mountain fold. Continue alternating these two folds for the desired length of the pleat fold. The folds can be stacked together or spread out to look like a fan.

Outside reverse fold

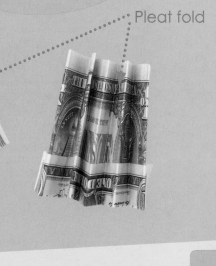

Pleat fold

DOLLAR BILL ARROW

You'll Need

✔ One dollar bill or play money

1 Place a dollar bill flat on a table. Bend the bottom left corner upward and align it with the top edge of the bill. Fold and make a crease. Unfold and repeat the process with the top left corner.

Fold up

Fold over

2 Unfold the bill. Lift the left edge, then bend it toward the middle. Align the bent end with the middle of the X mark created in Step 1. Fold and make a crease.

3 Unfold the bill. Lift the lower parts of the X-shape slightly and press them inward. You will see that Step 3 action caused the top part of the X-shape to lift up. Push the sides in and press the top down along the creases.

Push in

Press down

4 Lift the top part of the triangle created in Step 3. Bend the bottom part of the triangle along with the rest of the bill. Align with the middle of the triangle, fold and crease. Repeat with the other side of the bill.

5 Lift and bend the narrow end toward the arrow point. Align the bent end with the arrow head. Make sure that the bent end overlaps the arrow head by about 1/4 inch (0.5 cm). Fold and crease.

6 Slip the narrow end into the arrow point pouch. Turn it over. You have an arrow!

DOLLAR BILL AIRPLANE

You'll Need

✔ One dollar bill or play money
✔ Quarter

1 Place a dollar bill flat on a table. Fold the bill in half and make a crease.

2 Fold the bill in half again sideways and make a crease. Run a coin along the edge to make a sharp crease.

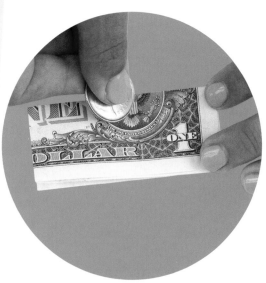

3 Unfold the second crease. Lift the right edge, then bend it toward the middle so that the bent end lines up with the crease line. Fold and make a crease.

4 Repeat Step 3 with the other side.

5 Lift the bottom right edge of the triangle. Bend it toward the middle so that the bent end aligns with the crease line. Fold and make a crease. Repeat with the other side.

6 Fold the triangle along the center crease created in Step 2.

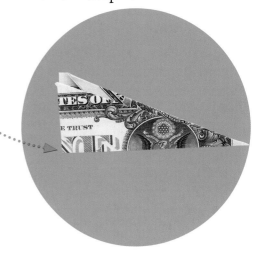

7 Fold the top corner of the triangle toward the bottom edge to form wings. Align the rest of the wing line along the edge. Fold and make a crease. Repeat with the other side.

8 Lift the wings up along the crease so they stick out and the plane can fly.

DOLLAR BILL RIBBON

You'll Need:

✔ One dollar bill or play money

1 Place a dollar bill flat on a table. Fold the bill in half as shown and make a crease.

2 Unfold the bill. Lift the top edge, bend it toward the middle, then align the bent end with the middle crease created in Step 1. Fold and make a crease. Repeat with the other half.

3 Lift the top right corner, then bend it toward the middle so that the bent end aligns with the middle crease line. Fold and make a crease. Repeat with the bottom right corner.

4 Repeat Step 3 with the other half of the bill.

5 Fold the bill along the crease from Step 1 to create a narrow band as shown.

6 Measure 1 1/2 inches (4 cm) from each tip of one end of the band. Make a tiny mark and fold the band along the line. It should bend in an angle.

7 Repeat Step 6 with the other end, but bend it in the opposite direction, across the first section.

DOLLAR BILL ENVELOPE

You'll Need:

✔ Two dollar bills or play money

1 Place a dollar bill flat on a table with the reverse side facing you upside down. Bend the top right corner downward and align it with the bottom edge of the bill. Fold and make a crease.

2 Bend the bottom left corner upward and align it with the top edge of the bill. Fold and make a crease.

Letter D

Letter R

3 Fold the bill in a straight line connecting letter R positioned near the bottom left edge and letter D positioned near the top right edge.

4 Make sure the bottom edges and the points are lined up properly.

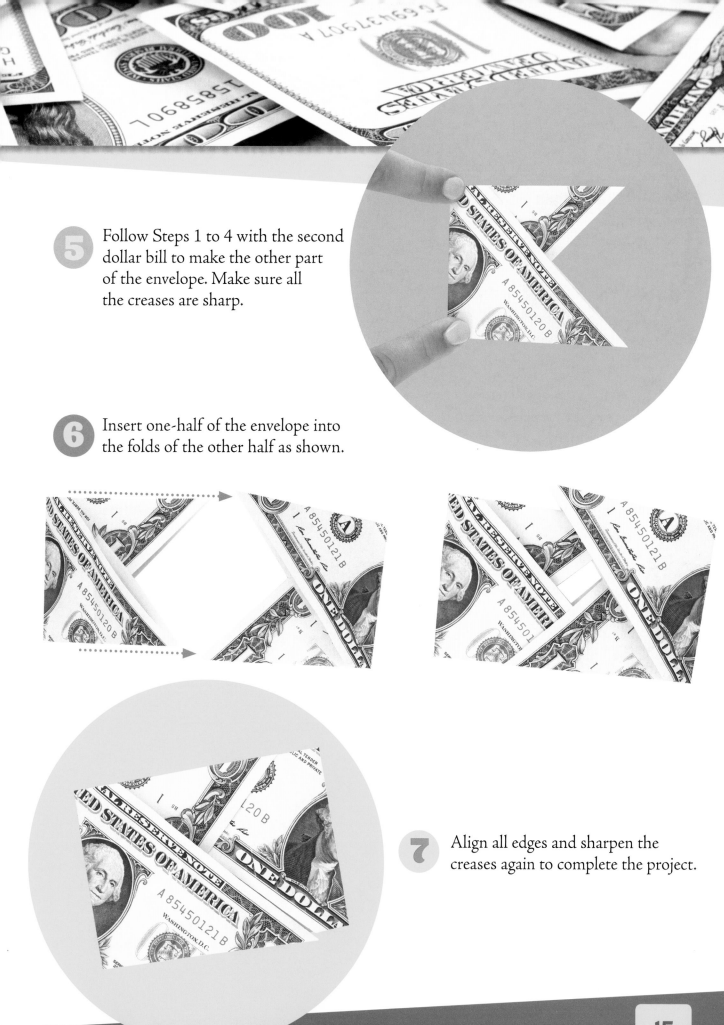

5 Follow Steps 1 to 4 with the second dollar bill to make the other part of the envelope. Make sure all the creases are sharp.

6 Insert one-half of the envelope into the folds of the other half as shown.

7 Align all edges and sharpen the creases again to complete the project.

DOLLAR BILL BOX

You'll Need
✔ Two dollar bills or play money

1. Place a dollar bill flat on a table. Lift and bend the left end upward and align it along the edges of the bill about 1 inch (2.5 cm) from the right edge of the bill. Fold and make a crease. Unfold and repeat the process with the right end.

2. Unfold the bill. Turn the bill face up. Lift the top edge, then bend it toward the middle. Align the bent end just above the number 1 graphic. Fold and make a crease.

Number 1 graphic

3. Lift the bottom edge, then align the bent end with the top side. Fold and make a crease.

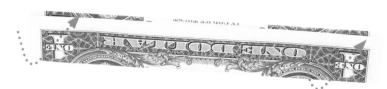

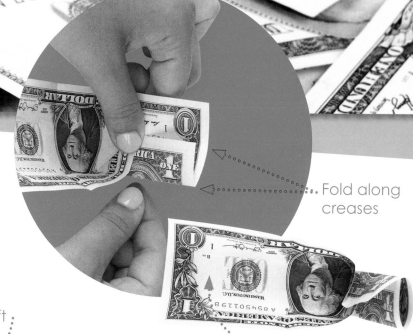

4 Unfold the bill. Hold one end of the bill and fold the end along the creases created in Steps 2 and 3 toward each other. Leave the other side of the bill unfolded.

Fold along creases

Leave unfolded

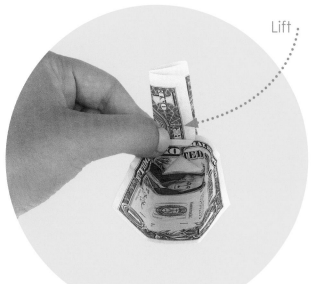

Lift

5 Lift the folded part at the crease created in Step 1. Tuck in the bottom corner to create the first side of the box.

6 Push the top part inside to reinforce the side.

Push in

7 Repeat Step 4 with the other half of the bill to complete the box. Make a second box to add a lid to your dollar bill box.

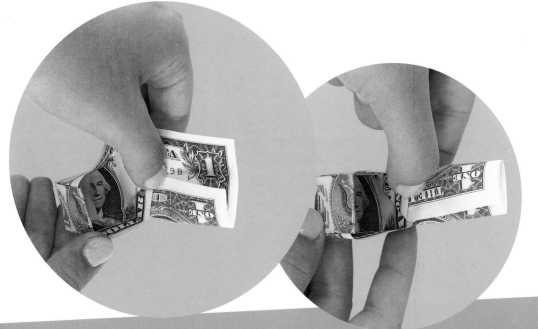

DOLLAR BILL HAT

You'll Need:

✔ One dollar bill or play money

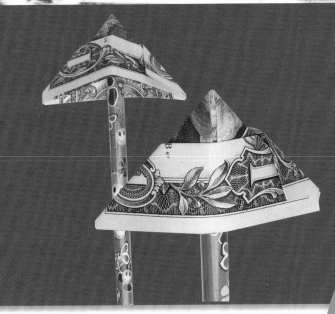

1. Place a dollar bill flat on a table. Fold the bill in half and make a crease.

2. Fold the bill in half again sideways and make a crease.

3. Turn the bill to have the folded edge on top. Lift the right corner of the folded end. Bend it toward the middle so that the bent end lines up with the middle crease line created in Step 2. Fold and make a crease. Repeat with the left corner.

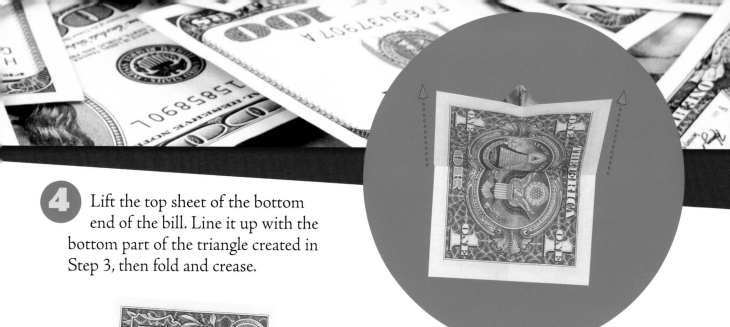

4 Lift the top sheet of the bottom end of the bill. Line it up with the bottom part of the triangle created in Step 3, then fold and crease.

5 Align the top part of the sheet with the bottom part, then fold and crease.

6 Turn the bill upside down and repeat Steps 4 and 5 with the bottom sheet.

7 Tuck the right corner of the front rectangle behind the triangle. Fold and crease. Tuck the right corner of the rectangle in the back over the folded front part. Fold and crease.

9 Unfold the bottom part to open the hat.

8 Repeat Step 7 for the left side in reverse order. Bend and crease the left corner of the back rectangle in front of the triangle. Tuck the left corner of the front rectangle over the folded back part.

DOLLAR BILL HOUSE

You'll Need:

✔ One dollar bill or play money

1 Place a dollar bill flat on a table. Fold the bill in half and make a crease.

2 Turn the bill to have the folded part on top. Fold the top corners into the center crease to form a point.

3 To create the chimney, lift the bottom corner of the left triangle. It needs to overlap the left edge of the triangle by about 1/4 inch (0.5 cm). Fold and crease.

4 Lift the right side of the bill, bend it inward about 1/4 inch (0.5 cm). Fold and crease.

5 Repeat Step 4 with the left side of the bill.

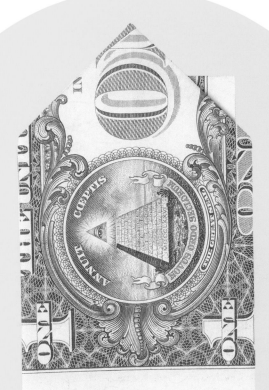

6 Lift the house and have it stand on its own. If it falls over, increase the bend in Steps 4 and 5.

DOLLAR BILL FAN

You'll Need:
✔ One dollar bill or play money

1 Place a dollar bill flat on a table. Lift the bottom edge of the bill, bend it inward about 1/2 inch (1 cm). Fold and crease.

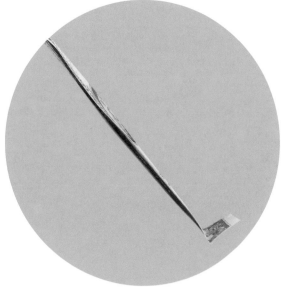

2 Turn the bill around. Lift the bottom edge of the bill, bend it inward about 1/2 inch (1 cm) to create a valley fold, fold and crease.

3 Push the bottom edge of the bill downward. Bend it about 1/2 inch (1 cm) to create a mountain fold, fold and crease.

Continue making a series of valley folds and mountain folds. This will create a pleat fold.

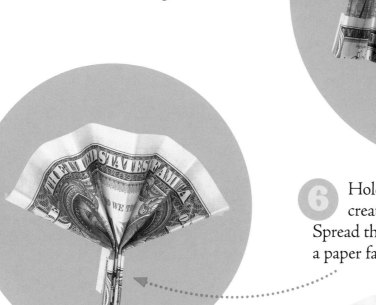

5 Push the sides of the bill together to form a folded rectangle.

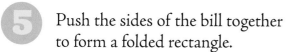

6 Hold the bottom end with the fold created in Step 1 firmly together. Spread the top edge apart to create a paper fan effect.

7 The bottom part might come slightly apart. Place the folded section under a heavy book, or wrap a rubber band around the base.

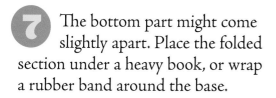

DOLLAR BILL SNAKE

You'll Need:

✔ 1 one dollar bill or play money

---

1 Place a dollar bill flat on a table. Lift the bottom edge of the bill, fold the bill in half and make a crease.

2 Unfold the bill. Lift the right corners. Bend them toward the middle so that the bent ends line up with the middle crease line. Fold and make a crease. Repeat with all corners.

3 Lift the bottom edge of the bill. Bend it toward the middle so that the bent end aligns with the middle crease line. Fold and make a crease. Repeat with the top edge.

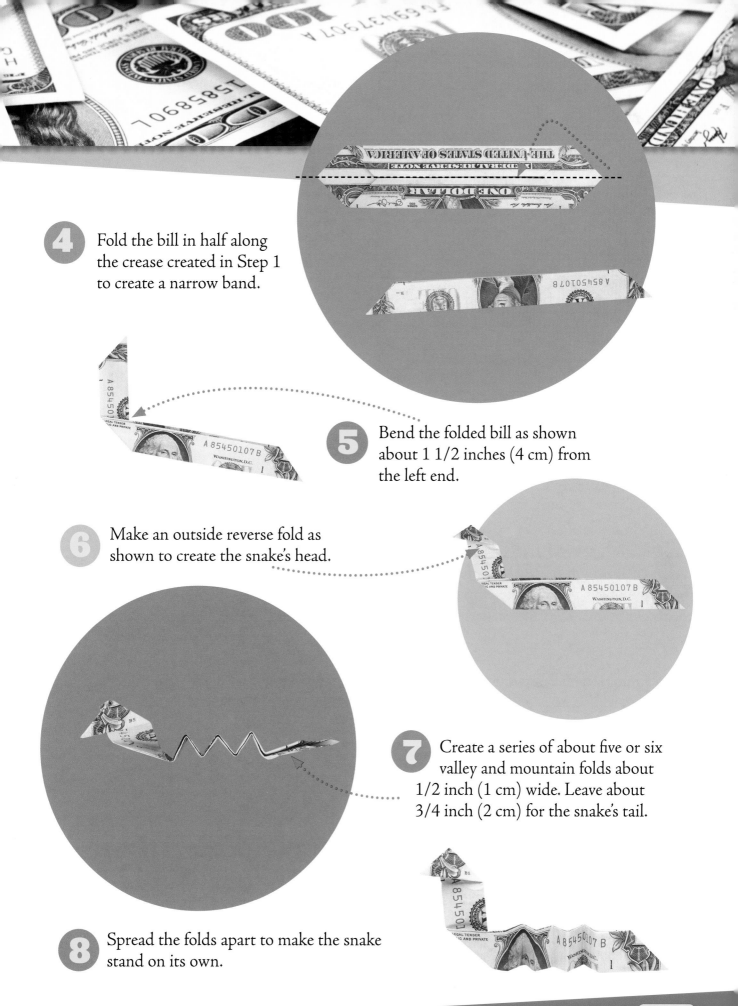

4 Fold the bill in half along the crease created in Step 1 to create a narrow band.

5 Bend the folded bill as shown about 1 1/2 inches (4 cm) from the left end.

6 Make an outside reverse fold as shown to create the snake's head.

7 Create a series of about five or six valley and mountain folds about 1/2 inch (1 cm) wide. Leave about 3/4 inch (2 cm) for the snake's tail.

8 Spread the folds apart to make the snake stand on its own.

DOLLAR BILL DOG

You'll Need:

✔ One dollar bill or play money

1 Place a dollar bill flat on a table. Bend the bottom left corner upward and align it with the top edge of the bill. Fold and make a crease. Unfold and repeat the process with the top left corner.

Fold up

2 Unfold the bill. Lift the left edge, then bend it toward the middle. Align the bent end with the middle of the X mark created in Step 1. Fold and make a crease.

Fold over

3 Unfold the bill. Lift the lower parts of the X-shape slightly and press them inward. You will see that Step 3 action caused the top part of the X-shape to lift up. Press the top down along the creases.

Push in

Press down

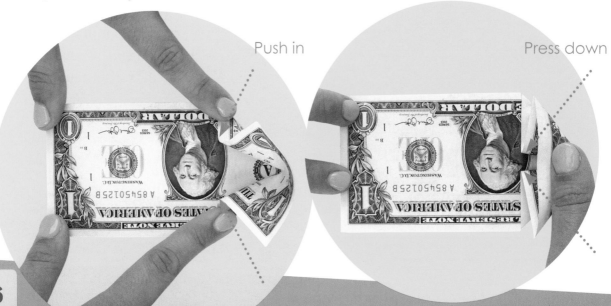

4 Lift and bend the straight bottom part downward and align it along the edges of the bill 1/2 inch (1 cm) from the top of the triangle. Fold and make a crease.

0.5 inch (1 cm)

5 Fold the bill in half again sideways and make a crease.

6 Lift the top parts of the triangle to create ears.

7 Bend the top corner of the ear downward. Align the edge with the top part of the body. Fold and crease. Repeat with the other ear.

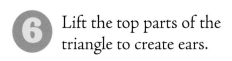

8 Spread the ears and the body fold apart so that the dog can stand on its own.

DOLLAR BILL HEART

You'll Need:

✔ One dollar bill or play money

1 Place a dollar bill flat on a table with the **obverse side** facing you. Fold the bill in half and make a crease.

2 Unfold the bill. Lift the left edge, then bend it toward the middle. Line up the bent end with the middle crease created in Step 1. Fold and make a crease. Repeat with the other half.

Flip over

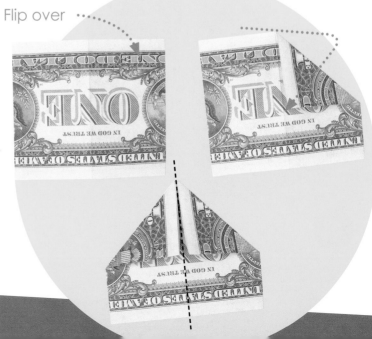

3 Flip the bill over. Lift the right top right corner. Bend it toward the middle so that the bent end lines up with the middle crease line. Fold and make a crease. Repeat with the left corner.

4 Fold the top leaf of the bottom edge toward the bottom of the triangle. Align the middle part with the triangle and crease.

Spread out into triangle

Straight edge

5 Follow the center crease, spreading out the outer sides into triangles. It is a little tricky to spread it into proper triangles. Take your time and be patient. Make sure that the edges of the triangle are straight.

6 Fold the center corners in as shown.

7 Flip the bill over and the heart is done.

DOLLAR BILL TREE

You'll Need:

✔ One dollar bill or play money

1 Place a dollar bill flat on a table. Bend the bottom left corner upward and align it with the top edge of the bill. Fold and make a crease. Unfold and repeat the step with the top left corner.

Fold up

2 Unfold the bill. Lift the lower parts of the X shape slightly and press them inward. You will see that Step 3 action caused the top part of the X shape to lift up. Push the sides in and press the top down along the creases.

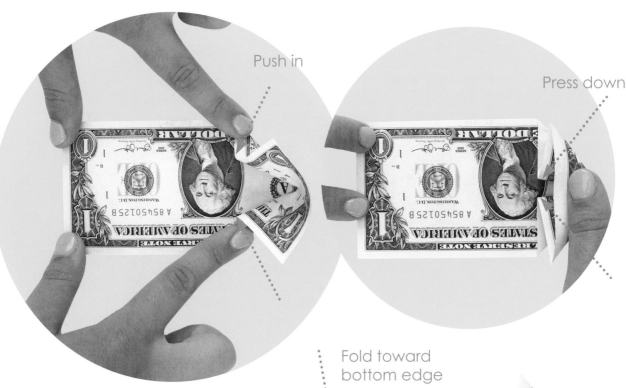

Push in

Press down

Fold toward bottom edge

3 Flip the bill over. Lift the top sheet, bend it toward the middle. Align the top edge with the bottom edge. Fold and crease.

4 Unfold the bill. Lift the bottom edge, then align it with the center crease from Step 3. Fold and crease. Repeat with the top edge.

5 Repeat Steps 1 and 2 with the narrow end of the bill.

6 Repeat Step 4 with the center part to make the tree trunk. Lift the bottom edge. Line it up with the center crease from Step 3. Fold and crease. Repeat with the top edge.

7 Bend the narrow tree trunk part, lifting the smaller triangle end above the wider triangle.

Slip on top

8 Slip the smaller triangle on top of the wider triangle. Adjust the length of the trunk to fit the triangular parts and press all parts firmly together to make the tree flat. Place the tree under a book for a few minutes if necessary to help it hold its shape.

GLOSSARY

elaborate Intricate and complex.

pulp A soft, wet material.

obverse side The front side of money bills.

three-dimensional Appearing to have length, width, and height.

two-dimensional Appearing to have length and width.

FOR MORE INFORMATION

Further Reading

Harbo, Christopher. *Origami Papertainment: Samurai, Owls, Ninja Stars, and More!*
North Mankato, MN: Capstone Press, 2015.

Owen, Ruth. *Kids Make Origami!*
New York: Windmill Books, 2016.

Rau, Dana Meachen. *Folding Origami.*
North Mankato, MN: Cherry Lake Publishing, 2014.

WEBSITES

For web resources related to the subject of this book, go to: www.windmillbooks.com/weblinks and select this book's title.

INDEX